Mental Aerobics
Grades 5-8

by Ann Fisher

illustrated by Marty Bucella

photo credit © Stockbyte™

cover by Jeff Van Kanegan

Publisher
Instructional Fair • TS Denison
Grand Rapids, Michigan 49544

ISBN: 1-56822-958-5
Mental Aerobics
Copyright © 2000 by Instructional Fair Group
a Tribune Education Company
3195 Wilson Dr. NW
Grand Rapids, Michigan 49544

Introduction

Staying physically fit has never been more popular or more important than it is today. An abundance of exercise videos, aerobics classes, and fitness programs are readily available almost everywhere. As a classroom teacher, however, you know that it is just as important to be in shape mentally as physically. The ability to think quickly and critically is an essential skill, one that needs to be practiced frequently in the classroom.

Your students will indeed get a mental workout as you pose the more than 400 questions in this book. *Mental Aerobics* is a book filled to capacity with busy brain benders, terrific trivia, perplexing puzzles, and important information. It will give those wandering minds some much-needed exercise!

This book is written in a "ready-to-use" format. Simply pick it up, open to any page, and read a question aloud to your students. Using only mental skills and computations, students will be challenged to think and respond quickly. No paper, worksheets, or pencils are required! It is an invaluable resource for those spare minutes between assignments or at the end of class periods, when you want to fill even a little time with a focused, worthwhile activity.

Mental Aerobics has been written for use in any classroom in the intermediate, upper, and even adult levels. Subjects covered vary widely, including everything from acronyms to anatomy, from metaphors to measurements. You will also find logic questions and general knowledge questions, making this the perfect resource for cross-curriculum classes. Throughout the book you will find a wide range of difficulty levels. If some questions seem too difficult or too easy for your group, simply skip over them. Remember: Since students are listening to the problems and doing all computations mentally, some questions may be harder than they appear.

Answers are included along with the questions for your quick reference. Some questions have precise answers, while others are open-ended. In these cases, possible answers are listed so you will be able to guide discussion and contribute sample solutions easily. Often extra background information is provided as well for your benefit. This book can also be the springboard for further research projects.

Hopefully, *Mental Aerobics* will become one of your favorite pieces of mental exercise equipment as you challenge your students to listen and think. Enjoy the workout!

How to Get the Most Out of This Book

Extend the learning. Some of the questions ask about historical facts, current populations, the top crop-producing countries, and so on. Sometimes, students will know the correct answers. In this case, challenge them to give even more details. For example, if they know the top two coffee-producing countries in the world, do they know the top five?
For some of the questions, students may not have any solutions. In these instances, you may wish to assign them as bonus research challenges. Students could be required to find the answers on their own time, even taking them home and asking their families for input.

Brainstorm. Some questions ask students to list a maximum number of answers to a particular problem. For these you may wish to record a composite list on the chalkboard, which can then be copied on paper and added to later. Whenever possible, allow time to discuss a wide variety of outcomes so that students are exposed to as many correct answers as possible.

Solve mathematical problems mentally. Many of the questions require mathematical computations. Read the question to yourself first to determine whether your students can solve it without paper and pencil. If so, do not allow them to write it down! However, if it is appropriate to have students jot down numbers or instructions, be certain that they have scrap paper and pencil ready.

Visualize geographical situations. Some questions concern bodies of waters, continents, foreign countries, and the United States. Encourage students to give their best answers without looking at a map. Then review correct solutions with them while they check their atlases.

1 An antique dealer bought a silver spoon for $5 and sold it for $6. He then bought the same spoon back for $7 and sold it for $8. How much profit did the dealer make in all?

Answer: $2 - He made $1 profit on the first transaction and another $1 on the second.

2 How many color words can you list that have no rhymes?

Possible answers: *purple, orange, silver, turquoise, aqua.*

3 List the nine planets of our solar system in alphabetical order.

Answer: Earth, Jupiter, Mars, Mercury, Neptune, Pluto, Saturn, Uranus, Venus

4 If you were to fly from Dublin to London to Paris, over which bodies of water would you travel?

Answer: the Irish Sea and the English Channel

5 Even numbers can be written as the sum of two primes. For example, the number 22 can be written as the sum of 3 + 19 or 11 + 11. Find two primes that will total each of these even numbers:
A. 20
B. 30
C. 40
D. 48

Answers: A. 7 + 13
                B. 11 + 19
                C. 17 + 23
                D. 19 + 29

6 How many ways can you win at tic-tac-toe?

Answer: 8 - There are three ways horizontally, three ways vertically, and two ways diagonally.

---

7 We use many words and phrases that contain references to the weather. For example, we ask for our eggs cooked *sunny-side-up*. Try to list at least five more similar weather phrases.

Possible answers: slush fund, stealing someone's thunder, a flood of applicants, brainstorming, a snow job, to shoot the breeze, etc.

8 Which of these cities is not in Canada?

A. Edmonton
B. Vancouver
C. Winnipeg
D. Duluth

Answer: D. Duluth is in Minnesota, in the United States.

---

9 After which war was the League of Nations formed?

Answer: World War I

---

10 Name all of the Seven Dwarfs.

Answer: Bashful, Sleepy, Dopey, Doc, Happy, Sneezy, Grumpy

11 What is the name of the style of the tall, silk hat often associated with Abraham Lincoln?

Answer: stovepipe

12 What country does not border on China?
A. India
B. Iran
C. Russia
D. Mongolia

Answer: B. Iran

13 In fiction, who was the character named Jacob Marley?

Answer: In Dicken's *A Christmas Carol*, he was the deceased partner of Ebenezer Scrooge.

14 A brother and a sister each have the same amount of money. How much should the sister give her brother so that he has ten dollars more than she does?

Answer: $5. (If she gave him $10, then he would have $20 more.)

15 A *chevron* would most likely be worn by someone in which of these professions?
A. doctor
B. soldier
C. priest
D. painter

Answer: B. soldier

16 Name at least four different types of drums.

Possible answers: tom-tom, snare, bass, timpani, conga, etc.

17 In what state is the world-famous Mayo Clinic?

Answer: It is in Minnesota, in the city of Rochester. It is a center for medical treatment that was founded by brothers William James Mayo and Charles Horace Mayo in 1889.

18 In a single-elimination soccer tournament with 16 teams, how many games will have to be played to determine the winning team?

Answer: 15; Fifteen teams have to be eliminated which requires 15 games.

How many games will the winning team have to play in this same tournament before it is declared the winner?

Answer: four games—In each of four rounds, half of the teams win. First eight teams win, then four teams, then two teams. In the fourth round just one team wins.

19 What is the name of the official retreat for the president of the United States, and where is it located?

Answer: Camp David is located in a heavily wood area of the Catoctin Mountains in Maryland.

20 Who was the first major-league baseball player to have his number retired?

Answer: Lou Gehrig, #4. He played his entire career for the New York Yankees. He was the first modern player to hit four home runs in one game. He also set the record for the most consecutive games played at 2,130.

21 How many lines are in a limerick, and which ones rhyme?

Answer: There are five lines. Lines 1, 2, and 5 rhyme with one another. Line 3 rhymes with line 4.

---

22 What single word can refer to a dark spot on the skin, a spy, and a small animal?

Answer: *mole*

---

23 How many keys are there in all on a piano? How many are black? How many are white?

Answer: There are 88 keys in all; 36 are black and 52 are white.

24 What European country is famous for its Waterford Crystal?

Answer: Waterford, Ireland, is the home of the Waterford Glassworks, which was founded in 1783 by brothers William and George Penrose. The hand-blown, lead oxide crystal is world-famous for its luster and the brilliance of its cutting. Waterford now exports a variety of items around the world, including tableware, chandeliers, and specially commissioned trophies.

---

25 Name the primary holy book for each of these groups of people:
A. Muslims
B. Christians
C. Jews

Answers: A. Koran
B. Bible
C. Torah

26 A train leaves Boston with 100 passengers. In New York, half the passengers get off and 35 more get on. In Philadelphia, 20 more passengers get on and no one gets off. In Washington, D.C., one fifth of the passengers get off. How many passengers are left to finish the journey to Atlanta?

Answer: 84. [(100 - 50 + 35 + 20)] - 21 = 84

27 What is the most common metallic element on earth?

Answer: Aluminum makes up 8.1% of the earth's crust by mass. It is the third most abundant element as well as the most abundant *metallic* element.

28 What is the most common nonmetallic element in the earth's crust?

Answer: Oxygen makes up almost 50% of the earth's crust by mass. It also forms about 21% (by volume) of the atmosphere.

29 Which of these South American countries is located the farthest north?
A. Argentina
B. Brazil
C. Peru
D. Venezuela

Answer: D. Venezuela

30 People in what profession would use a hammer and tongs?

Answer: blacksmith

31 Many interesting words in the English language contain the letters in *jack.* Name a word with *jack* for each definition I give.
A. breakfast food
B. a very versatile person
C. woodsman
D. a big prize

Answer: A. *flapjacks*
B. *jack-of-all-trades*
C. *lumberjack*
D. *jackpot*

32 In seagoing language, what is the opposite of *port?*

Answer: starboard. As you face the front of a boat, *port* is the term for the left side and *starboard* is the term for the right side.

33 Give the famous literary name for each author's real name:
A. Theodor Geisel
B. Samuel Langhorne Clemens
C. Charles Lutwidge Dodgson

Answers: A. Dr. Seuss
B. Mark Twain
C. Lewis Carroll

34 Where is the world's largest coral reef?

Answer: The Great Barrier Reef is off the coast of Australia. It is a chain of coral reefs and islands about 1,250 miles long.

35 The number of people in a football stadium doubles every ten minutes. After an hour, the stadium is full. When was the stadium half full?

Answer: after 50 minutes

36 Which of these states does not share a border with Arizona?

A. California
B. Texas
C. Utah
D. New Mexico

Answer: B. Texas

---

37 Name five or more different types of quadrilaterals.

Answers: square, rectangle, trapezoid, parallelogram, rhombus, and kite.

---

38 In which sport is the Heisman trophy awarded?

Answer: college football. The award is given each year to the outstanding college football player in the United States. It was first awarded in 1935, and it is named after John W. Heisman, who was a leading football coach from 1892 to 1927.

39 In baseball, one team scored six runs in one inning. What is the minimum number of batters that went to the plate that inning?

Answer: 9—There were the six batters who scored plus three more who made the team's three outs.

What is the maximum number of batters that would have gone to the plate in that same inning?

Answer: 12—There were the six who scored, the three who made outs, and three more who could have been stranded on base.

---

40 Which fruit shares a name with a flightless bird?

Answer: kiwi (The bird is a native of New Zealand.)

41 How many words of one syllable can you spell that contain more than six letters?

Possible answers: *screeched, straight, strength*

---

42 What is the name of the world's longest dogsled race, and where is it held?

Answer: The Iditarod takes place in March every year in Alaska, from Anchorage to Nome. The race covers 1,159 miles and lasts over a period of several days.

43 Name three Jewish holidays.

Answers: Hanukkah, Rosh Hashanah, and Yom Kippur.

---

44 A picture frame's outer dimensions are 12" x 20". If the frame is 1 inch wide all the way around, what is the area of the print inside the frame?

Answer: 180 sq. in. (The print is 10" x 18".)

---

45 Name the common six-letter word that can be spelled using the letters in lap and ten.

Answer: planet

---

46 In what European country would you find the Vistula, Oder, and Narew Rivers?

Answer: Poland

47 A bottle filled with perfume sold for $20. The perfume was then emptied out and priced separately from the bottle. The bottle was then valued at a price that was $19 higher than the perfume. What was the value of just the perfume?

Answer: The perfume was worth 50 cents; the bottle was worth $19.50.

48 Name the two men who served as vice presidents under President Richard Nixon.

Answer: Spiro Agnew and Gerald Ford

49 List at least five words that rhyme with *pocket.*

Answers: *locket, socket, docket, rocket, sprocket.*

50 When and where did the Six-Day War take place?

Answer: The Six-Day War occurred in 1967 in the Middle East. The fighting was between Israel and nearby Arab countries over disputed territories. The United Nations arranged a cease-fire, which ended the war after six days.

51 Riddle: What tree is dressed the warmest?

Answer: the fir (fur)

52 The British Parliament is made up of the Queen and what other two bodies?

Answer: the House of Commons and the House of Lords. The House of Commons has 635 elected members and holds virtually all the power. The House of Lords has about 1,150 members, but most take no active part in governmental proceedings.

53 Translate this inflated sentence into a well-known proverb: An excess number of culinary experts will diminish the quality of the simmering liquid entree.

Answer: Too many cooks spoil the broth.

54 What single word can precede each of these to form three compound words?
A. work, town, stretch
B. brow, glasses, sore
C. block, map, way

Answers: A. *home*
　　　　　B. *eye*
　　　　　C. *road*

55 How often does a sesquicentennial event occur?

Answer: once every 150 years

56 The Japanese poetry form known as haiku must contain how many syllables?

Answer: 17—There are 5 in the first and last lines and 7 in the middle line.

57 Bryce plants a young tree that has a diameter of one inch. For each of the next five years the tree grows a ring that is a quarter-inch thick. What will the tree's diameter be at the end of five years?

Answer: 3½ inches. Each ¼-inch ring adds ½ inch to the diameter of the tree. Adding 2½ inches to the original 1-inch diameter yields a total size of 3½ inches.

58 Which of the five Great Lakes is located farthest east? Which is farthest north?

Answers: Ontario is farthest east; Superior is farthest north.

59 What famous aviator first broke the sound barrier in 1947?

Answer: Chuck Yeager was the first person to fly an aircraft faster than the speed of sound. He did this on October 14, 1947, in a Bell X-1 rocket airplane. In 1953 he broke another record by flying two-and-a-half times the speed of sound in a Bell X-1A.

60 Name five or more words that function as both nouns and verbs.

Possible answers: *run, bank, score, count, list, bat,* etc.

61 Which country is incorrectly matched with its capital?
A. Greece - Athens
B. Portugal - Lisbon
C. Switzerland - Vienna
D. Ireland - Dublin

Answer: C. Switzerland's capital is Bern. Vienna is the capital of Austria.

62 Aunt Agatha likes only certain numbers. She likes 2, 5, 7, 23, and 31. She doesn't like 4, 6, 21, and 30. Name three more numbers that Aunt Agatha likes.

Answer: Any prime numbers are acceptable, such as 11, 13, 17, 19, 29 and so on.

63 Name two words that rhyme for each of the following phrases. Hint: All the answers will be one-syllable words.

A. immaculate female ruler
B. strange whiskers
C. someone who steals cows
D. song about dried fruit

Answers: A. *clean queen*
B. *weird beard*
C. *beef thief*
D. *prune tune*

64 Where are the NATO headquarters located?

Answer: in Brussels, Belgium. Belgium was one of the original 12 nations who signed the North Atlantic Treaty in 1949. (The other 11 countries were Canada, Denmark, France, Great Britain, Iceland, Italy, Luxembourg, the Netherlands, Norway, Portugal, and the United States. Other countries signed the treaty in subsequent years.)

65 Name the two major islands off the coast of Italy.

Answer: Sicily and Sardinia

66 I have five brothers and each of my brothers has one sister. How many children are in my family?

There are two possible answers:
1. There are six people if the speaker is a girl, the one sister.
2. There are seven people if the speaker is a boy. There would be five brothers, a sister, and himself.

67 A symphony orchestra uses more of one instrument than any other. What is it?

Answer: The violin is used most because more violins are needed to balance the corresponding viola, cello, and bass sections.

68 We use many phrases that include items of clothing. For example, we might speak of having something *up our sleeve*, or having *a bee in our bonnet*. Try to list at least three other such phrases that mention articles of clothing.

Possible answers: fits like a glove, living on a shoestring, to hit below the belt, too big for his britches, a big wig, etc.

69 Where is your *uvula?*

Answer: in your mouth. It is the small piece of flesh which hangs above the back of your tongue.

70 Name the first 13 perfect square numbers.

Answer: 1, 4, 9, 16, 25, 36, 49, 64, 81, 100, 121, 144, 169

71 Who ran against George Bush in the 1988 U.S. presidential election?

Answer: Michael Dukakis

72 What is the name of the vegetable that looks like a tiny head of cabbage?

Answer: brussel sprouts

73 In what country would you find Oxford and Cambridge Universities?

Answer: Great Britain

74 What kind of animals do each of these scientists study?

A. ichthyologist
B. apiculturist
C. entomologist
D. ornithologist

Answers: A. fish
B. bees
C. insects
D. birds

75 Hannah's hash contains 3 parts of beef for every 4 parts of potato. If Hannah wants to make a total of 21 pounds of hash, how many pounds of meat and potatoes does she need?

Answer: 9 pounds of beef and 12 pounds of potatoes.

76 In children's fiction, what is the name of the 10-year-old boy who can solve any mystery?

Answer: Encyclopedia Brown is the hero created by author Donald Sobol. The twenty-plus volumes featuring Encyclopedia include *Encyclopedia Brown Gets His Man*, *Encyclopedia Brown Saves the Day*, and *Encyclopedia Brown and the Case of the Disgusting Sneakers*.

77 Who was the first gymnast to score a perfect "10" in the Olympics, and which country did she represent?

Answer: Nadia Comaneci from Romania was awarded 7 perfect tens at the 1976 Olympics in Montreal.

78 Name the four basic golf clubs.

Answer: iron, driver, putter, wedge

79 Which body of water does not border on Africa?

A. Mediterranean Sea
B. Black Sea
C. Atlantic Ocean
D. Indian Ocean

Answer: B. Black Sea

---

80 Who won baseball's first World Series, and when was it played?

Answer: The Boston Red Sox of the American League beat the National League Pittsburgh team five games to three in 1903. The World Series has been played every year since 1903, with the exception of 1904.

81 What Arabic numeral is represented by the Roman numeral MCMLXXVI?

Answer: 1976

82 What is the American name for these European terms?

A. candy floss
B. biscuit
C. car boot
D. dressing gown

Answers: A. cotton candy
         B. cookie
         C. car trunk
         D. bath robe

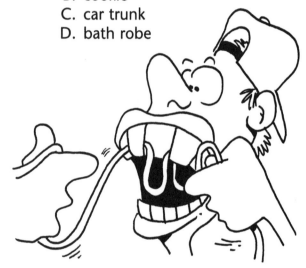

83 Which is not a characteristic of amphibians?

A. cold-blooded
B. live births
C. moist skin
D. three-chambered heart

Answer: B. Most amphibians lay eggs in the water.

84 Which "Peanuts" character plays classical piano music?

Answer: Schroeder

---

85 Who said, "Genius is 99% perspiration and 1% inspiration"?

Answer: Thomas Edison

---

86 Which country does not share a border with France?
A. Spain
B. Portugal
C. Italy
D. Germany

Answer: B. Portugal

87 Many common English words contain the letters *dog*. Give a *dog* word or phrase for each definition that I read to you:
A. a kind of tree
B. shabby and worn
C. used for identification

Answers: A. *dogwood*
B. *dog-eared*
C. *dog tag*

---

88 Name two musical instruments that use a vibrating reed.

Answers: oboe, clarinet, saxophone, and bassoon

89 Jack has two containers of quarters totaling $10. The pail in his left hand contains $3 more than the pail in his right hand. How many quarters are in each pail?

Answer: The pail on the left must contain $6.50, or 26 quarters. The pail on the right contains $3.50, or 14 quarters.

90 How many three-cent stamps are in a dozen?

Answer: There are always 12 stamps in one dozen.

91 Name at least four authors who are known by some of their initials rather than their full name.

Possible answers: A. A. Milne, e. e. cummings, E. B. White, J. R. R. Tolkien, C. S. Lewis, O. Henry, H. G. Wells, E. L. Doctorow

92
A. Germany was divided into two countries, East and West Germany, after which war?
B. What was the capital of each country?
C. What year was Germany reunified?
D. What is the capital of Germany now?

Answers: A. World War II
B. West Germany, Bonn; East Germany, East Berlin
C. 1990
D. Berlin

93 What does the cooking term *sauté* mean?

Answer: to fry rapidly in butter

94 What single word can follow each of these to complete three compound words?

A. play, back, under
B. turn, make, left
C. touch, show, hoe

Answers: A. *ground*
B. *over*
C. *down*

---

95 How would you describe a day with a temperature of 20°C?

A. freezing cold
B. chilly
C. mild and lovely
D. very hot

Answer: C. 20°C is equal to 68°F.

96 In a fictional children's story, who lives in the Hundred Acre Wood?

Answer: Winnie-the-Pooh

---

97 The Smith family is planning a long journey of 3,600 miles. They plan to drive 200 miles the first day, 400 miles the second day, and 600 miles the third day. Then they will repeat the three-day pattern until their journey is over. How many days will the Smiths be traveling?

Answer: nine days. In each three-day segment they will travel 1,200 miles. They need to do that three times (for a total of nine days) to go 3,600 miles.

---

98 Gluten is a nutritious substance found in what crop?

Answer: It is found in wheat. *Gluten* is the collective term for the major protein components in wheat.

99 Into what body of water does the Nile River empty?

Answer: the Mediterranean Sea

---

100 In Monopoly, which color of property brings the highest rent?

Answer: The dark blue properties generate the most rent. The rental on Park Place is $35, and on Boardwalk the fee is $50.

---

101 What kind of animal has a crop?

Answer: a bird. Its crop is often called a gizzard. It is an enlargement of the esophagus used for food storage.

102 Which one of these common childhood illnesses is not caused by a virus?
A. measles   C. mumps
B. chicken pox   D. whooping cough

Answer: D. Whooping cough, or pertussis, is caused by bacteria.

---

103 How many legs would there be

A. in a crowd of 300 bipeds?
B. in a herd of 300 quadrupeds?
C. in a group of 300 centipedes?

Answers: A. 300 x 2 = 600
             B. 300 x 4 = 1,200
             C. 300 x 100 = 30,000

104 The expression "Slow but steady wins the race" comes from which one of Aesop's fables?

Answer: The Tortoise and the Hare

105 Name three Canadian cities that have over one million people.

Possible answers: Toronto, Montreal, Vancouver, and Ottawa/Hull

106 Which city is not a major city in Ireland?
A. Dublin
B. Limerick
C. Liverpool
D. Cork

Answer: C. Liverpool is a city in England.

107 In a church, what part is the foyer? What is the chancel?

Answer: The foyer is the entrance hall; the chancel is usually where the choir sits.

108 What is the name of Bill and Hillary Clinton's pet cat?

Answer: Socks

109 How many two-digit whole numbers are there?

Answer: 90. Consider all the numbers from 1 to 99. There are 99, of which the nine numbers from 1 to 9 have just one digit. That leaves 90 two-digit numbers.

110 Translate this inflated sentence into a well-known proverb: A pair of errors do not constitute a single rectitude.

Answer: Two wrongs don't make a right.

111 What country grows the most:

A. corn?
B. rice?
C. tea?

Answers:
A. The United States grows about ⅖ of the world's supply of corn, chiefly in the Midwest region known as the corn belt.
B. China grows about ¾ of the world's crop of rice.
C. India produces about 1.5 billion pounds of tea each year. China is second with a yield of about 1 billion pounds.

112 According to "Frosty the Snowman," what object gave life to the snowman?

Answer: an old silk hat

113 Name two words that rhyme for each of the following phrases. Hint: All the answers will be two-syllable words.

A. improved cardigan
B. basement resident
C. skinny dart
D. careful scholar

Answer: A. *better sweater*
          B. *cellar dweller*
          C. *narrow arrow*
          D. *prudent student*

114 What is the space or distance between two musical pitches called?

Answer: interval

115 Which vegetable plant is a perennial?

A. carrot   B. beet
C. radish   D. asparagus

Answer: D. asparagus (A perennial is a plant that lives for more than two years.)

116 What would you study if you were a speleologist?

Answer: caves. The study of caves is called *speleology*.

117 Amber scored 20 points in last night's basketball game. If she made 3 free throws and 3 three-pointers, how many two-point goals did she make?

Answer: 4

118 The first televised U.S. presidential debate was in 1960. Who were the two candidates in that debate?

Answer: Kennedy and Nixon

119 Which country does not border on the Red Sea?
A. Egypt   C. Ethiopia
B. Saudi Arabia   D. Turkey

Answer: D. Turkey

120 What were the names of the seven children on the television program *The Waltons*?

Answer: John-Boy, Mary Ellen, Jason, Ben, Erin, Jim-Bob, Elizabeth

121 What kind of animals live in an apiary? What kind of animals live in an aviary?

Answer: bees; birds

122 Two hundred people were asked whether they preferred regular, diet, or classic Fruit Fiz pop. Responses showed that 10% preferred diet and 20% preferred regular. What number of people chose classic?

Answer: 140 people (70%)

123 Who was George Bush's vice president? What state was he from?

Answer: Dan Quayle; Indiana

124 What is *turmeric?*

Answer: a spice

125 Many common English words begin with the letters *bill*. Name a *bill* word or phrase for each of these definitions:
  A. a very large number
  B. a game played with balls on a table
  C. a farm animal

Answers: A. *billion*
          B. *billiards*
          C. *billy goat*

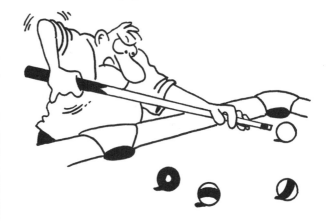

126 How many times can you subtract 5 from 25?

Answer: once. After that the number is 20.

127 We use many phrases that contain a part of the body. For example, we talk about the *heart of a matter* or *giving someone the cold shoulder*. List at least four more phrases that include a part of the body.

Possible answers: a thumbnail sketch, a bone of contention, turn the other cheek, kick up your heels, wet behind the ears, etc.

128 Which of these is not considered to be an allegory?
A. *Pilgrim's Progress*
B. *Gone with the Wind*
C. *Animal Farm*

Answer: B. *Gone with the Wind*
An allegory is a story in which fictional characters and events symbolize larger truths or generalizations.

129 Which athlete has been on the cover of *Sports Illustrated* a record 31 times?

Answer: Muhammad Ali, the former world heavyweight boxing champion

130 How many teeth are in a normal adult mouth?

Answer: 32

131 Name at least four root vegetables.

Possible answers: beet, turnip, radish, carrot, rutabaga, horseradish, sweet potato, and parsnip

132 What is the name of the longest bone in the human body, and where is it located?

Answer: The femur is located in the thigh. It is about 20 inches long in a person who is 6' tall.

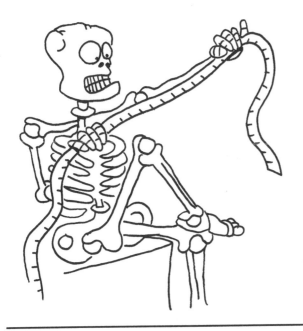

133 In children's fiction, what is the name of the six-year-old who attends boarding school in Paris and is both brave and naughty?

Answer: Madeline is the character created by author Ludwig Bemelmans. The well-known first lines in most of the Madeline books are, "In an old house in Paris that was covered with vines lived twelve little girls in two straight lines."

134 What single word can follow each of these to complete three compound words?
A. space, battle, court
B. back, cup, over
C. row, tug, steam

Answers: A. *ship*
  B. *board*
  C. *boat*

135 Who invented both the alcohol and mercury thermometers?

Answer: Daniel Fahrenheit

136 A rectangular box measures exactly 72 cubic feet. What are its possible dimensions? Give 3 answers.

Answers: 3 x 3 x 8
  6 x 4 x 3
  12 x 2 x 3

137 What country celebrates its founding every year on July 1?

Answer: Canada. On July 1, Canada celebrates its founding in 1867, and the day is called Canada Day or Dominion Day.

---

138 Into what body of water does the Mississippi River empty?

Answer: the Gulf of Mexico

---

139 Aunt Agatha likes only certain numbers. Today she likes 18, 24, 15, 57, 36, and 60. She doesn't like 6, 22, 31, 40, and 102. Name three more numbers Aunt Agatha likes.

Answer: Any two-digit multiples of 3 are acceptable such as 21, 27, 33, 48, 72, etc.

140 What is the ingredient that gives jams, jellies, and preserves their smooth, semi-solid consistency?

Answer: pectin

---

141 Which state does not share a border with Georgia?
A. Florida
B. Tennessee
C. South Carolina
D. Virginia

Answer: D. Virginia

142 Using only the letters in *pocket*, spell at least six words of four letters.

Possible answers: *cope, poke, poet, peck, pock, tock*

143 What word names a Mexican state and a spicy sauce?

Answer: *Tabasco*

144 What is the U.S. state that is divided into two separate parts by a large body of water?

Answer: Michigan—Lake Michigan separates the Upper Peninsula from the Lower Peninsula.

145 How many two-digit whole numbers contain at least one 7?

Answer: 18 numbers; 17, 27, 37, 47, 57, 67, 70, 71, 72, 73, 74, 75, 76, 77, 78, 79, 87, 97

146 Name the three green properties on a Monopoly board.

Answer: Pennsylvania Avenue, North Carolina Avenue, Pacific Avenue

147 What country was once known as Persia?

Answer: The name *Persia* was given by the Greeks to a large area of land in southwestern Asia which is now known as Iran and Afghanistan.

148 What kind of food would you serve from a tureen?

Answer: soup

149 Name two novels written by Jack London.

Possible answers: *The Call of the Wild*, *White Fang*, and *The Sea-Wolf*

150 A pet shop owner has 3 parrots, and twice as many parakeets. He also has 8 cockatiels. He also has 10 rabbits, 2 turtles, 4 gerbils, 12 dogs, and 12 cats. How many birds does he have in all?

Answer: 17 birds—3 parrots, 6 parakeets, and 8 cockatiels

151 What is the main function of a tree's fruit?
A. store energy
B. protect seed
C. fertilize seed
D. absorb nutrients

Answer: B. to protect the seed

152 What six-letter word can be spelled using the letters in these word pairs?

A. cue + fat

B. elm + owl

C. red + war

Answers: A. *faucet*
         B. *mellow*
         C. *drawer*

---

153 A person in what profession would use a baton, a score, a podium, and a metronome?

Possible answer: orchestra conductor. A baton is the stick used for directing the group; a score is the conductor's copy of music that shows each instrument's part; a podium is the raised platform on which the conductor stands; the metronome is an instrument that gives a steady rhythm at variable speeds.

154 What was the name of the first English child born in America, and where was she born?

Answer: Virginia Dare was born on Roanoke Island, North Carolina, in 1587.

---

155 What percentage of air is made up of oxygen?

Answer: 21% (78% is made up of nitrogen. Argon and other gases make up the other 1%.)

---

156 The sum of two numbers is 24. Their product is 80. What are the two numbers?

Answer: 20 and 4

157 Name the three largest cities in Alaska.

Answer: According to the 1990 census, Anchorage 226,338; Fairbanks 30,843; Juneau 26,751

158 Give the year that each of these wars began and ended:
A. American Revolutionary War
B. American Civil War
C. World War I

Answer: A. 1775–1783
          B. 1861–1865
          C. 1914–1918

159 How would you say "thank you"

A. in French?
B. in Spanish?
C. in German?

Answers: A. merci
           B. gracias
           C. danke

160 How long is an international nautical mile?

Answer: 6,076.115 feet, or 1,852 meters

161 What is the former name of the city of Istanbul?

Answer: Constantinople was the city's official name until 1930.

162 What country does not border on Iraq?

A. Russia   C. Turkey
B. Iran   D. Saudi Arabia

Answer: A. Russia

---

163 What does a numismatist do?

Answer: He or she collects coins. *Numismatics* is the study or collecting of coins, paper money, medals, etc.

---

164 List five words that come before *able* in the dictionary.

Possible answers: *aardvark, abacus, abduct, abhor, abbreviate, ability*, etc.

165 Who is the author of *Where the Sidewalk Ends* and *A Light in the Attic?*

Answer: Shel Silverstein

---

166 Translate each inflated sentence into a well-known proverb:
A. It is futile to attempt to instruct a canine of many years with innovative maneuvers.
B. Members of a winged species with identical plumage congregate.

Answers: A. You can't teach an old dog new tricks.
B. Birds of a feather flock together.

167 Greg trades three quirks for one blob. Joshua trades two zoogs for one quirk. If Elizabeth wants to trade six zoogs, how many blobs should she receive?

Answer: one

---

168 What does an anemometer measure?

Answer: It measures wind speed. The most common type has three or four cone-shaped cups at the end of rods. This unit rotates on an upright spindle. The faster the wind blows, the faster the cups rotate. The wind speed is measured by the number of revolutions in a given period of time and is registered on a dial on the anemometer.

169 Place these fasteners in order, according to when they were first used: zipper, button, velcro, safety pin.

Answer: button (1200), safety pin (1849), zipper (1893), velcro (1957)

---

170 Ten states in the United States have reached all-time record high temperatures of 120° F or higher. Can you guess which ones?

Answer: Arizona, Arkansas, California, Kansas, Nevada, North Dakota, Oklahoma, South Dakota, Texas, New Mexico

171 What do the letters in the U.S. governmental group EPA stand for?

Answer: Environmental Protection Agency

172 About how far is the sun from the earth?

Answer: about 93 million miles

173 A cat and dog together weigh 20 pounds. The dog weighs three times as much as the cat. How much does each animal weigh?

Answer: The dog weighs 15 pounds, and the cat weighs 5 pounds.

174 Name the state with each of these nicknames:
A. Beaver State
B. Hoosier State
C. Badger State
D. Land of Opportunity

Answers: A. Oregon
B. Indiana
C. Wisconsin
D. Arkansas

175 When was Halley's comet last seen from the earth? When should it be seen again?

Answer: It was last seen in 1986. It is expected to be in view again in 2061.

176 Who was the only bachelor to serve as U.S. president?

Answer: James Buchanan

177 How many players are on an official

A. baseball team?
B. American football team?
C. volleyball team?
D. soccer team?
E. ice hockey team?

Answers: A. 9   D. 11
          B. 11   E. 6
          C. 6

178 Which amendment to the U.S. Constitution gave 18-year-olds the right to vote, and when was it passed?

Answer: It was the Twenty-Sixth Amendment, passed in 1971.

179 Through which English town does the prime meridian pass?

Answer: Greenwich, England. It was the site of the Royal Greenwich Observatory from 1675 to 1958. The building contains a brass strip marking the prime meridian (zero degrees longitude). It is now part of the National Maritime Museum.

180 Give the Roman numeral for 769.

Answer: DCCLXIX

181 In what year did the *Titanic* sink? About how many people died?

Answer: 1912; about 1,500

182 Name two words that rhyme for each definition I read. Hint: Each word in the answer contains three syllables.
A. yellow fruit from Cuba
B. a debate about drums
C. little bits of long noodles

Answer: A. *Havana banana*
B. *percussion discussion*
C. *spaghetti confetti*

---

183 Into what body of water does the Amazon River empty?

Answer: Atlantic Ocean

---

184 What fairy-tale character is destroyed after his name is mentioned?

Answer: Rumplestiltskin

185 What word can you place in each blank to complete a familiar item or phrase?
_____ setter, _____ coffee, _____ linen

Answer: Irish

186 Give examples of how the word *short* can be used as a noun, adjective, and verb.

Possible answers:
noun—The electrical wiring had a short in it.
adjective—The clown was very short.
verb—The cashier is trained not to short her customers.

187 Cathy has one dollar to spend at the candy store. Lollipops are 25 cents each, chocolates are 10 cents each, and toffees are 5 cents each. If Cathy buys two lollipops, how many toffees can she get?

Answer: 10 toffees

188 What is the angle of the earth's axis of rotation?

Answer: 23.5 degrees

189 Where is Three Mile Island, and why is it famous?

Answer: It is in Pennsylvania. On March 28, 1979, the worst accident in U.S. nuclear reactor history occurred there.

190 Which states in the United States have the highest populations? Name the top five in order.

Answer:
1. California
2. New York
3. Texas
4. Florida
5. Pennsylvania

191 What toy is made of 87 feet of flat wire coiled into a 3-inch-diameter circle that stands 2 inches high when stacked?

Answer: the Slinky. It was invented in 1945 by Richard James of Philadelphia.

192 What is the name of a geographical dictionary or index that contains the names of places and their locations in alphabetical order?

Answer: a gazetteer

193 List at least six words that contain three letters of the alphabet in consecutive order.

Possible answers: *defend, defeat, hijack, inoperative, inopportune, stuck, stupendous,* etc.

194 What is the common name for the cardiac muscle?

Answer: heart

195 A mother is 49, and her daughter is 19. How many years ago was the mother three times as old as her daughter?

Answer: four years ago, when the mother was 45 and the daughter was 15

196 Which British queen ruled the British Empire longer than any other monarch? How long did she reign?

Answers: Queen Victoria ruled for 64 years, beginning in 1837.

197 What is the driest continent?

Answer: Antarctica. Although it is largely snow-covered, the cold air holds so little moisture that annual precipitation totals only a few inches in most places.

198 Ninety-eight percent of the world's crayfish come from which state in the United States?

Answer: Louisiana

199 Can you name the person whose portrait appears on these U.S. bills?
A. one-dollar bill
B. five-dollar bill
C. ten-dollar bill
D. twenty-dollar bill
E. fifty-dollar bill
F. one hundred-dollar bill

Answers: A. George Washington
B. Abraham Lincoln
C. Alexander Hamilton
D. Andrew Jackson
E. Ulysses S. Grant
F. Benjamin Franklin

200 What language is spoken by more people than any other?

Answer: Mandarin Chinese. It is spoken by 885 million people.

201 Which package holds more?
Package A is 4" x 5" x 5".
Package B is 8" x 6" x 2".

Answer: Package A holds more. It holds 100 cubic inches, while B holds 96 cubic inches.

202 Give the correct name for each of these people in a courtroom.

A. the police officer who maintains order

B. the person who types every word that is said during the trial

C. the person who accuses another and brings the lawsuit to court

D. the person who is accused of a crime and is being tried

Answer: A. bailiff
B. court reporter
C. plaintiff
D. defendant

WHAM!

203 What is the largest saltwater lake in the world? What is the largest freshwater lake?

Answers: The Caspian Sea is the largest saltwater lake; Lake Superior is the largest freshwater lake.

204 Who is eligible to win the Purple Heart?

Answer: Anyone serving in the U.S. armed forces who is wounded in combat is eligible.

205 A clock reads 10:45 a.m. when the power goes off for 1 hour and 53 minutes. At what time should the clock be reset?

Answer: 12:38 p.m.

206 What is the focus of the study of *gerontology*?

Answer: aging

207 What single word can precede each of these to complete three compound words?

A. bill, writing, out
B. drop, bow, coat
C. man, ball, flake

Answer: A. *hand*
         B. *rain*
         C. *snow*

---

208 In what country is Mount Olympus?

Answer: Greece

---

209 In what state is the highest mountain peak in the continental U.S. located?

Answer: California. Mt. Whitney is 14,494 feet tall.

210 Suppose that four people in your family each take five showers a week, and that each shower lasts for ten minutes. If your shower uses six gallons of water per minute, how many gallons of water does your family use for showers in one week?

Answer: 1,200 gallons

---

211 What is the smallest display element on a video display screen?

Answer: a pixel, which is an acronym for picture element

212 Which is not a country in South America?

A. Peru   C. French Guiana
B. Bolivia D. Cameroon

Answer: D. Cameroon is in Africa.

---

213 What award is given to the illustrator of the most distinguished children's picture book in a certain year?

Answer: The Caldecott Medal is named after an English illustrator of children's books. Two past winners include Maurice Sendak in 1964 for *Where the Wild Things Are* and Chris Van Allsburg in 1982 for *Jumanji*.

---

214 Farmer Phil has 100 animals. He has 25 chickens, 15 cows, and the rest are sheep. What fraction tells how many of his animals are sheep?

Answer in lowest terms: ⅗

215 What was the magic phrase that Ali Baba used to open the cave of the 40 thieves?

Answer: "Open Sesame" was the magic password.

216 Name the seven days of the week in alphabetical order.

Answer: Friday, Monday, Saturday, Sunday, Thursday, Tuesday, Wednesday

217 Which of these upper case block letters would look the same in a mirror?
M H N L W I T B A

Answer: M H W I T A

---

218 What do the letters in NASA stand for?

Answer: National Aeronautics and Space Administration

---

219 Rearrange the letters in *supersonic* to spell a category of musical instruments.

Answer: percussion

---

220 Two factory workers, Burly and Curly, each work at different speeds on different shifts. Burly works a 6-hour shift and makes 12 parts per hour. Curly works an 8-hour shift and makes 10 parts per hour.
  A. In one shift, which worker makes the most parts?
  B. In one shift how many parts do the two workers make altogether?
  C. In 24 hours of work time, how many parts do the two workers make altogether?

Answer:
A: Curly makes more
B: 152 parts (6 x 12) + (8 x 10)
C: 528 parts (6 x 12 x 4) + (8 x 10 x 3)

---

221 How many three-letter words can you spell using only the letters in *turkey*?

Possible answers: *key, rut, yet, try, rye, rue, yuk*

222 What one word can mean both "a great number" and "one who entertains guests"?

Answer: *host*

---

223 What is a *troy* weight used to measure?

Answer: It is used to weigh precious metals such as gold and silver. It is based on a pound of 12 ounces.

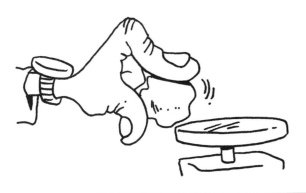

---

224 Place these methods of transportation in order, according to when each was invented: tractor, automobile, bicycle, steam locomotive, diesel truck, cable streetcar

Answer: bicycle (1791), steam locomotive (1803), cable streetcar (1874), automobile (1885), tractor (1892), diesel truck (1924)

225 If you had a ten-dollar bill, could you afford to buy a $12 shirt that was on clearance for 20% off if you live in a state that has 5% sales tax?

Answer: no. The shirt would cost $9.60, but with the sales tax, the total would be $10.08.

226 When is the official Atlantic hurricane season?

Answer: from June 1 through November 30

227 Anna Mary Moses is better known as Grandma Moses. For what is she famous?

Answer: She was an artist who lived from 1860–1961. She painted mostly landscapes and childhood scenes. She never had a painting lesson in her life, and she used ordinary, inexpensive materials.

---

228 Which amendment to the U.S. Constitution
   A. abolished slavery?
   B. gave women the right to vote?
   C. guarantees freedom of religion?

Answers: A. Thirteenth
          B. Nineteenth
          C. First

---

229 What is the area and perimeter of a square whose sides are each 7 cm long?

Answers: The area is 49 square centimeters; the perimeter is 28 centimeters.

230 We use many phrases that contain a musical word. For example, we talk about *jumping on the bandwagon* or *harping on a subject.* Try to list at least five more musical phrases.

Possible answers: play second fiddle, an upbeat attitude, a keynote speaker, blowing your own trumpet, and don't give me a song and a dance

---

231 Who was the first vice president of the United States? Who was the second?

Answers: John Adams was the first; Thomas Jefferson was the second.

232 Name a national capital that the Nile River flows through.

Answer: Cairo, Egypt, or Khartoum, Sudan

---

233 Name two words that rhyme for each definition I read. Hint: All the answers will have two syllables.
A. sluggish flower
B. pasta for a small dog
C. fastener for sheep
D. horrible pair

Answers: A. *lazy daisy*
B. *poodle noodle*
C. *mutton button*
D. *gruesome twosome*

---

234 How many six-ounce glasses of juice can be poured from a three-pound bottle?

Answer: 8 glasses

235 Who are *garbologists?*

Answer: scientists who study, measure, and weigh things that people throw away in an effort to find better ways to dispose of garbage

236 Which planet in our solar system is the largest? Smallest?

Answer: Jupiter is the largest, with a diameter of nearly 89,000 miles; Pluto is the smallest, with a diameter of about 1,400 miles.

237 Tell the starting and ending dates for these wars:

A. World War II   B. Korean War

Answers: A. 1939–1945
          B. 1950–1953

---

238 Name the three largest cities in California.

Answer: According to the 1999 almanac using 1996 population estimates, the three cities and their populations are Los Angeles—3.5 million, San Diego—1.1 million, and San Jose—839,000. The larger metropolitan areas of all three have much higher populations.

---

239 Which of these three events has the lowest probability?

A. rolling a number lower than 4 on a die
B. rolling a number higher than 4 on a die
C. rolling an odd number on a die

Answer: B. The chances of rolling a 5 or a 6 are ⅓. The chances of the other events are ½.

240 Where is the longest underground cave in the world?

Answer: The Mammoth-Flint cave system in Kentucky is 300 miles long.

ENTER AT YOUR OWN RISK.

241 The properties on the Monopoly board game are actual street names in what U.S. city?

Answer: Atlantic City, New Jersey

242 Yesterday was four days before Halloween. What will be the date tomorrow?

Answer: October 29

---

243 What relation are each of these to you:

A. your mother's brother's daughter
B. your sister's grandson
C. your mother-in-law's granddaughter
D. your mother's son's daughter

Answers: A. your cousin
        B. your great nephew
        C. your niece or daughter
        D. your niece

244 What name is given to the words on a map that explain the symbols that are used?

Answer: the legend

---

245 What is the difference between a *short ton* (commonly used in the United States and Canada) and a *long ton (or metric ton)* commonly used in Great Britain?

Answer: A short ton is 2,000 pounds. The long ton, or metric ton, is 1,000 kilograms, or 2,240 pounds.

---

246 Finish this proverb by Benjamin Franklin: *Well done is better than ...*

Answer: *well said.*

247 A. Who was the first president to take office following the death of the previous president?

Answer: John Tyler became president in April 1841. His predecessor, William Henry Harrison, caught cold while giving the longest inaugural speech and died one month later.

B. Seven presidents since William Harrison have also died in office. Can you name them?

Answer: In order they are: Zachary Taylor, Abraham Lincoln, James Garfield, William McKinley, Warren Harding, Franklin Roosevelt, and John Kennedy.

---

248 Think of two words that sound the same but have two different meanings for each set of definitions.
   A. much above average in size, and a metal framework that holds fuel in a fireplace
   B. an amount of material to be learned at one time, and to reduce the quantity of something

Answers: A. *great* and *grate*
             B. *lesson* and *lessen*

249 What important U.S. or world event occurred on each of these dates?
A. July 20, 1969
B. August 9, 1974
C. April 15, 1912

Answers:
   A. Astronauts Neil Armstrong and Edwin Aldrin became the first men to walk on the moon.
   B. Richard Nixon became the first U.S. president to resign from office.
   C. *Titanic* sank after colliding with an iceberg, killing 1,517 people aboard.

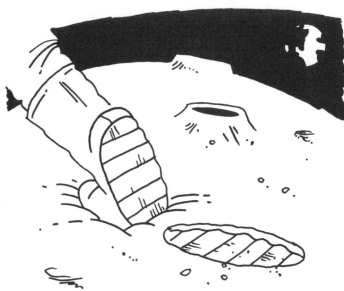

---

250 How can you write four 9s so that they equal 100?

Possible answer: 99%

251 For each famous athlete, name the sport in which he participated and the last team for which he played.
  A. Wilt Chamberlain
  B. Yogi Berra
  C. Jim Brown
  D. Gordie Howe

Answers: A. basketball, Los Angeles Lakers
          B. baseball, New York Yankees
          C. football, Cleveland Browns
          D. ice hockey, Detroit Red Wings

252 Name the three largest cities in Pennsylvania.

Answer: According to the 1990 census, the three largest cities and their populations are Philadelphia—1.6 million, Pittsburgh—370,000, and Erie—109,000. The larger metropolitan areas of all three have much higher populations.

253 What are CFCs?

Answer: CFC stands for *chlorofluorocarbons*. They are man-made gases that contain chlorine, fluorine, and carbon. They are found in aerosol cans, refrigerator coolants, and air conditioners. It is thought that they destroy the ozone layer of the earth's atmosphere.

254 How many 6-inch pieces of rope can be cut from a mile-long rope?

Answer: 10,560 pieces. There are 5,280 feet in a mile, and two pieces can be cut from each foot.

255 Where is the world's highest waterfall?

Answer: Venezuela is home of Angel Falls, which is 3,212 feet high.

256 Which is not a country in Asia?

A. Indonesia   C. Haiti
B. Malaysia   D. Burma

Answer: C. Haiti is in North America.

---

257 Who was the first American woman in space? What year did she first travel in space?

Answer: Sally Ride in 1983, at the age of 32

---

258 The busiest shipping port in the world is in Rotterdam. It handles 350 million metric tons of goods per year. In what country is this port located?

Answer: Netherlands

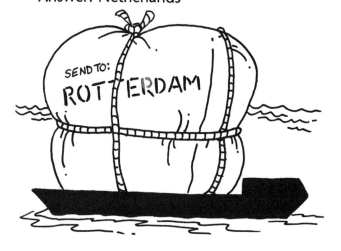

259 Overdue library fines at one library are 10 cents per day per book and 5 cents per day per magazine. Polly just returned 3 books and 3 magazines that were one week late. How much does she owe the library?

Answer: $3.15 [(7 x 3 x .10) + (7 x 3 x .05)]

260 Can you name the top three fruit crops in the world?

Answers: 1. oranges—annual production of about 58 million metric tons
2. bananas—annual production of about 54.5 million metric tons
3. grapes—annual production of just over 53 million metric tons

261 According to calls to one automobile association, a list was made of the most common causes of car breakdowns. Can you name the top three reasons given?

Answers: 1. battery problems
2. tire problems
3. keys (locked out of car, difficulties with the security system, etc.)

262 A pair of standard dice is rolled so that a sum of 11 appears on the top. What sum would be shown on the bottom of this pair?

Answer: Three. Opposite sides on a pair of dice always total 7: 1 + 6, 2 + 5, 3 + 4. If a pair of dice totals 11, the top sides would have to be 6 and 5, so the bottom sides must be 1 and 2, for a total of 3.

263 This baseball team was first known as the Alleghenies, after the nearby Allegheny River. But in the 1890s they earned a new nickname after they stole players from another baseball club. What is the current name of this baseball team?

Answer: the Pittsburgh Pirates

264 Finish these quotes by Abraham Lincoln:
A. The best way to destroy your enemy is to make him . . . .
B. The ballot is stronger than . . . .

Answers: A. your friend
B. the bullet

265 Which U.S. city has the most police officers?

Answer: New York City has the most of any city with over 37,000. Chicago ranks second with just over 13,000 officers.

266 Which statement is true?

A. The word *noun* is a pronoun.
B. The word *verb* is a noun.
C. The word *adjective* is a verb.

Answer: B. Any part of speech is the name of an object and, therefore, a noun.

267 General Motors is the U.S. company that makes the greatest profit—$218 per second. At this rate, about how much profit does GM make in one minute? In one hour?

Answers: In one minute, first round 218 to 220 and then multiply by 60, the number of seconds per minute. The profit is about $13,200 per minute. In one hour, round the profit per minute to $13,000 and multiply by 60, the number of minutes in an hour. The profit is about $780,000 per hour.

268 Name the three largest cities in Europe.

Answer:
1. Moscow, Russia—pop. 10,769,000
2. London, United Kingdom—pop. 8,897,000
3. Paris, France—pop. 8,764,000

269 In the history of U.S. presidents, three sets of men have been related to one another. Can you name the people and explain how they were related?

Answers:
1. John Adams and John Quincy Adams were father and son.
2. William Henry Harrison and Benjamin Harrison were grandfather and grandson.
3. Theodore Roosevelt and Franklin Roosevelt were cousins.

270 Where did Orville Wright's famous first flight take place?

Answer: Kitty Hawk, North Carolina. It was on December 17, 1903, and it lasted for 12 seconds.

271 Name five beverages manufactured by the Coca-Cola Company other than Coca-Cola.

Possible answers: Fanta, Sprite, Tab, Fresca, Mr. Pibb, Hi-C soft drinks, Mello Yello, Diet Coke, and Ramblin' Root Beer

272 What country has the longest coastline in the world?

Answer: Canada has the longest, 151,485 miles. Indonesia ranks second with just 33,999.

273 Which country does not border on the Mediterranean Sea?
A. Austria   C. Algeria
B. France   D. Libya

Answer: Austria does not touch the Mediterranean. It is landlocked.

274 One store is offering two special promotions during the Christmas season. Promotion A gives you $5 off any purchase totalling $20 to $99. Promotion B gives you 5% off any purchase. Which is the better deal?

Answer: Promotion A offers 5.05% to 25% which is better than Promotion B's discount of 5%.

275 Many common English words begin with the letters *cat*. Name a *cat* word for each of these definitions:

A. a classification
B. a disaster
C. a marsh plant
D. a descriptive booklet of items for sale

Answers: A. *category*
B. *catastrophe*
C. *cattail*
D. *catalog*

276 The difference between two numbers is 5. Their product is 36. What are the two numbers?

Answer: 4 and 9

277 What holiday song is the top-selling single of all time around the world?

Answer: "White Christmas" by Bing Crosby has sold over 30 million copies.

278 Name at least four famous American comedy teams.

Possible answers: the Marx brothers, the Three Stooges, Laurel and Hardy, Abbott and Costello, Burns and Allen, and Rowan and Martin

279 What is the longest river in Europe?

Answer: The Volga is 2,290 miles long and flows through Russia.

IF19312 Mental Aerobics

280 If odd numbers are kumquats and even numbers are oranges,
A. what is an kumquat plus a kumquat?
B. what is an orange plus an orange?
C. what is an orange plus a kumquat?

Answers: A. orange
B. orange
C. kumquat

---

281 What country consumes more tea per person than any other in the world?

Answer: Republic of Ireland is first, averaging 1,390 cups per person per year. The United Kingdom is second with 1,113 cups.

282 List three words that come after *zoo* in the dictionary.

Possible answers: *zoology, zoom,* and *zucchini*

283 Can you name the five most popular candies in the United States? (Be specific.)

Answers:
1. Reese's Peanut Butter Cup with 5.0% of the market share
2. Snickers Original with 4.8%
3. M & M Plain with 3.5 %
4. M & M Peanut with 3.2 %
5. Hershey's KitKat with 2.4 %

---

284 What professional basketball team has won the most NBA titles?

Answer: The Boston Celtics have won the title 16 times.

285 List four mistakes in this paragraph:

Two days ago it was Easter Sunday. All the children was busy hunting for eggs and candy. One little boy, Bobby, found the most highest number of eggs. Tomorrow, on Thursday, he will share the eggs with three children who are in the hospital suffering with ammonia.

Answers:
1. The second sentence should say, "All the children *were . . . .*"
2. *Most highest number* should read simply, *most.*
3. Today must be Tuesday, so tomorrow should be Wednesday.
4. The correct name of the illness is *pneumonia.*

286 Becky has 50 blue and white marbles. Thirty-five of them are blue. What percentage of Becky's marbles are white?

Answer: Thirty percent of the marbles are white.

287 Tell which state in the United States is known by each of these nicknames:
A. Hawkeye State
B. Prairie State
C. Garden State
D. Beehive State

Answers: A. Iowa
B. Illinois
C. New Jersey
D. Utah

288 Where is the world's largest active volcano?

Answer: Hawaii. The Mauna Loa rises to more than 13,650 feet above sea level.

289 Which of these famous people would be the oldest if he/she were alive today? Which would be the youngest?

A. Elvis Presley
B. John F. Kennedy
C. Marilyn Monroe
D. Martin Luther King, Jr.

Answers: JFK was born in 1917, making him the oldest of the group. Presley was born 1935, making him the youngest. Monroe was born in 1926, and King was born in 1929.

290 Into what body of water does the Volga River empty?

Answer: the Caspian Sea

291 What single word can have both of these meanings:

A. a deep affection
B. a score of nothing

Answer: *love* (zero in tennis)

292 What is the perimeter of an octagon where each side is 11 inches long?

Answer: 88 inches

293 Where is the world's largest reference library? What is it called?

Answer: The Library of Congress in Washington, D.C., contains about 29 million books. The second largest is the British Library in London, which contains just over 20 million books.

294 **A.** What does it mean to *impeach* a president of the United States?

Answer: To impeach a president is to charge him/her with committing a crime or misdemeanor in office. It results in a trial in which he/she can be acquitted or found guilty.

B. What is the only governmental body that can impeach the president?

Answer: The House of Representatives

C. Who are the only two U.S. presidents to be impeached?

Answer: Andrew Johnson (1868) and William Clinton (1998)

---

295 How long are each of these measurements?
A. fathom
B. rod
C. furlong

Answers: A. 6 feet
             B. 5.5 yards
             C. 40 rods or 220 yards

296 List the seven continents of the world in order from largest to smallest.

Answer: Asia, Africa, North America, South America, Antarctica, Europe, Australia

---

297 In what profession would someone use a zester, a colander, and a tenderizer?

Answer: A cook or a chef would use these. A *zester* is a tool used to grate lemon peel, a *colander* is a strainer, and a *tenderizer* is either a substance or a tool used to make meat easier to chew.

TOSS HIM A **ZESTER**, THEN A **COLANDER** AND FINISH HIM OFF WITH A **TENDERIZER!**

298 Give five examples of deciduous trees.

Possible answers: any that lose their leaves once a year, including maple, oak, locust, birch, poplar, and fruit trees.

299 Arlene works at the Candy Counter. Yesterday she sold 5 boxes of chocolate that each weighed ½ pound and four boxes of licorice that each weighed ¾ pound. How many pounds of candy did Arlene sell in all?

Answer: 5½ pounds (She sold 2½ pounds of chocolate and 3 pounds of licorice.)

300 According to the U.S. Constitution, who holds the power to declare war?

Answer: Article 1, Section 8, vests this power in Congress, but the Supreme Court has ruled that the president may recognize a "state of war" initiated against the United States by a foreign power or by a domestic rebellion.

301 For what is Johannes Gutenberg well-known?

Answer: He was a pioneer in the use of movable type. The Gutenberg Bible, printed some time between 1450 and 1456, is the first volume known to have been printed with movable metal type.

302 What is the name of the most prestigious bicycle race in the world?

Answer: the Tour de France. It was founded in 1903, and the first race covered 1,510 miles. The longest Tour de France was held in Belgium in 1926 and covered 3,570 miles.

303 Max, the secret agent, fears he is about to be held hostage by the enemy in a room with a four-digit security code. He gets word to his associate just in time that he will undoubtedly be able to learn the security code which he will try to relay to his partner in a cryptic message. If given the opportunity, Max says he will relay the four digits in a message but warns that none of the digits will be in the proper place, lest his hidden motive become too obvious.

A. Sure enough, Max gets trapped. At the first opportunity he sends this message outside with his captors, which his partner is able to intercept:

All is well at 15:33 hours. Signed, Max

What is the highest number of security codes Max's partner will need to try before breaking him out?

Answer: only two. Since the two 3s are in the third and fourth position, and since Max indicated NO digits would be in their correct places, we know that the 3s must be in the first two positions. That means the only possible combinations are 3315 and 3351. Good work, Max!

B. Suppose the same thing happens again, but this time the enemy uses a three-digit code. Max sends out this notice:

Send supper at 7:15.

How many different codes are now possible?

Answer: two, 571 and 157

---

304 From the outside, the human brain appears as three distinct, but connected parts, one of which is the brain stem. Can you name the other two?

Answer: the cerebellum and the cerebrum

305 What is the last name shared by the three English novelists, sisters Charlotte, Emily, and Anne?

Answer: Brontë. The sisters were born in 1816, 1818, and 1820 respectively. Some of their best-known works were:
Charlotte—*Jane Eyre*
Emily—*Wuthering Heights*
Anne—*Agnes Grey*

306 Can you list three well-known suspension bridges in the United States?

Possible answers: The Brooklyn Bridge in New York City, opened in 1883; The Golden Gate Bridge in San Francisco, completed in 1937; and the Mackinac Bridge in Michigan, opened in 1958. There are others as well.

307 In which sentence is the word *verb* used as a verb?
A. The store sold verbs and nouns.
B. Lucy wore a verb sweater.
C. Tommy will verb the entire apple.

Answer: sentence C. In A, it is used as a noun; in B it is used as an adjective.

308 How many women's names can you list that begin with the letter J?

Possible answers: Jan, Jane, Janet, Janelle, Janice, Joan, JoAnne, Jill, Jillian, Jenny, Jennifer, Jessica, June, Joy, Jody, Judy, Joyce, Jaqueline, and Jerri

309 In what year was Desert Storm fought? Who was the U.S. president at that time?

Answers: Desert Storm was fought in 1991, under the direction of President Bush.

310 A library charges a circulation fee of $1.00 per video, 50 cents per CD, and 25 cents per cassette. Ronan wants to check out 5 CDs and 6 cassettes. How much money will he need?

Answer: $4.00 [(5 x .50) + (6 x .25)]

311 How are tendons and ligaments alike? How are they different?

Answers: Both are strong connective tissue made of the protein collagen. Tendons join muscle to bone; ligaments join bone to bone.

312 Which Canadian province is directly north of the state of Washington?

Answer: British Columbia

313 In what city would you find the longest underground railway network in the world?

Answer: London. The "Tube" system first opened in 1863. It now has 270 stations and 251 miles of track. The New York City system is just slightly shorter with 249 miles of track.

314 Neil Armstrong was the first man to walk on the moon. What was the name of the spacecraft that took him there?

Answer: *Apollo 11*

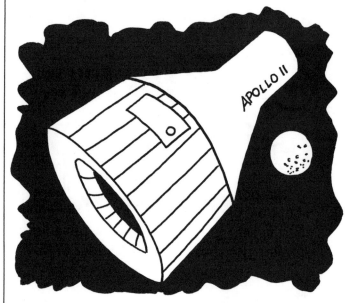

315 A set of three standard dice is rolled so that the sum of the numbers on top is 10. What is the sum of the numbers shown on the bottom of these three dice?

Answer: The sum of opposite sides of one die is always 7, so for three dice the sum would be 21. Since the top numbers equal 10, the bottom numbers have to equal 11.

---

316 The best-selling car of all time was first produced in 1937. What model was it?

Answer: the Volkswagen Beetle. It is estimated that over 21 million have been made.

317 What country has the most

A. pigs?
B. turkeys?
C. camels?

Answers:
A. China has the most pigs, nearly 425 million. The United States ranks second with about 60 million.
B. The United States leads the world in turkeys with about 88 million. France is second with about 36 million.
C. Somalia has the most camels (about 6.2 million), while Sudan comes in second with about 2.9 million.

318 Which state does not share a border with Michigan?
A. Wisconsin   C. Minnesota
B. Indiana   D. Ohio

Answer: Minnesota. Michigan's Upper Peninsula shares a border with northern Wisconsin, but not Minnesota.

319 We use many phrases that contain color words. For example, we say that something happens once in a *blue* moon or giving someone the *red-carpet* treatment. List at least four more colorful phrases.

Possible answers: every cloud has a silver lining; painting the town red, silence is golden, blue-chip stocks, being green with envy, etc.

320 What is the base-ten number for this Roman numeral? MMMCDLIX

Answer: 3,459

321 Name the three largest cities in Ohio.

Answer: According to the 1999 almanac, using 1996 population estimates, Columbus—657,000, Cleveland—498,000, and Cincinnati—346,000. The larger metropolitan areas of all three have much higher populations

322 What is the largest bird in the world? What is the smallest?

Answers: The ostrich is the largest. It can weigh up to 345 pounds and stand as high as 8 feet tall. The bee hummingbird, which lives in Cuba, is the smallest bird. It measures only 2.5 inches long at maturity. Newly hatched ones are just the size of honeybees.

323 Name the 12 months of the year in alphabetical order.

Answer: April, August, December, February, January, July, June, March, May, November, October, September

324 What major world event occurred on each of these dates?
A. November 22, 1963
B. January 28, 1986
C. December 7, 1941

Answers:
A. John F. Kennedy was assassinated in Dallas, Texas.
B. The *Challenger* space shuttle exploded 73 seconds after take-off, killing all 7 crew members.
C. The Japanese attacked Pearl Harbor, forcing the United States into World War II.

325 What three countries produce the most garbage in the world?

Answer: The United States leads the list, producing over 1,600 pounds per person per year. Australia ranks second with 1,520 pounds, and Canada is third with about 1,450 pounds per person per year.

326 If even numbers are zucchini, and odd numbers are radishes,
A. what is a radish multiplied by a radish?
B. what is a zucchini multiplied by a zucchini?
C. what is a radish multiplied by a zucchini?

Answers: A. radish B. zucchini C. zucchini

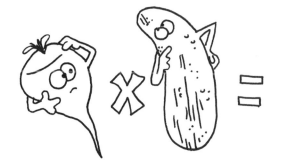

327 Where is the world's busiest airport?

Answer: Chicago's O'Hare airport is the busiest with nearly 67 million passengers per year.

328 What is Europe's busiest airport?

Answer: London's Heathrow airport has over 51 million passengers per year.

329 A rectangle has an area of 36 square feet. Give five possible measurements for its perimeter.

Answers:
A. If the rectangle is 2' x 18', its perimeter is 40 feet.
B. If the rectangle is 3' x 12', its perimeter is 30 feet.
C. If the rectangle is 4' x 9', its perimeter is 26 feet.
D. If the rectangle is 6' x 6', its perimeter is 24 feet.
E. If the rectangle is 36' x 1', its perimeter is 74 feet.

---

330 How many three-letter words can you spell using only the letters in *radish?* (Do not use plurals.)

Possible answers: *aid, air, had, has, hid, rid, sad, sir, his*

How many four-letter words can you form without using plurals?

Possible answers: *arid, dash, dish, hair, hard, raid, rash, said, sari*

331 The Detroit Lions play in one of the largest NFL stadiums. It has a capacity of over 80,000 people. What is the name of the stadium?

Answer: the Pontiac Silverdome

---

332 In the periodic table of the elements, hydrogen is the first element. Its atomic number is 1, and its symbol is H. What element is next, with an atomic number of 2? What is its symbol?

Answers: Helium is second in the table, and its symbol is He.

333 Which of the following cities are *not* located on the Gulf of Mexico? New Orleans, Corpus Christi, Dallas, Galveston, Jacksonville, Tampa

Answer: Dallas and Jacksonville are not. Dallas is inland from the Gulf; Jacksonville is on the Atlantic coast of Florida rather than the Gulf coast.

334 What is the surface area of a 9-cm cube?

Answer: 486 sq. cm (6 sides x 9 cm x 9 cm)

335 For what is Fort Knox, Kentucky, well-known?

Answer: It is a U.S. Army post and gold depository. The U.S. Treasury gold bullion vaults were built there in 1937.

336 What government agency oversees all broadcasting in the United States?

Answer: The Federal Communications Commission (FCC) is an independent government agency made up of seven members who are appointed to seven-year terms by the president. They are responsible for radio and television broadcasting, telephone communication, and communication satellites.

337 Translate each inflated sentence into a well-known proverb.
A. It is fruitless to shed tears due to outpoured dairy fluid.
B. It's impossible to estimate the value of a bound publication from its exterior.

Answers:
A. Don't cry over spilled milk.
B. You can't judge a book by its cover.

338 What is the top coffee-producing country in the world?

Answer: Brazil is the top coffee producer. The second highest producer is Colombia.

339 If A = 1, B = 2, C = 3, D = 4, etc., what is the value of these words?
A. DAB
B. BABY
C. CABBAGE

Answers:
A. 7 (4+1+2)
B. 30 (2+1+2+25)
C. 21 (3+1+2+2+1+7+5)

340 What is a *zephyr*?

Answer: a gentle breeze

341 What is *perjury*?

Answer: It is the offense of deliberately making a false statement under oath when appearing as a witness in legal proceedings on a point that is material to the question at issue.

342 A *marsupial* is a mammal in which the female has a pouch where she carries young. How many marsupials can you name?

Possible answers: kangaroos, wallabies, opossum, wombats, bandicoots, koalas, and others

343 The high temperature one winter day in Marquette, Michigan, was -20°F. The next day it was 0°F, and on the third day it was 14°F. What was the average temperature in Marquette for those three days?

Answer: -2°F (-20° + 0° + 14°) ÷ 3 = -2°

344 What one word has both of these meanings?
A. an aromatic plant
B. a place where coins are stamped under governmental authority

Answer: *mint*

345 How many kinds of squash can you name?

Possible answers: zucchini, acorn, buttercup, butternut, spaghetti, hubbard, pumpkin, and others

346 Which is greater, 25% of 80 or 20% of 90?

Answer: 25% of 80 is the greater. It equals 20, while 20% of 90 is only 18.

347 In the United States, the official mint is the Bureau of the Mint, which is a division of the Treasury Department. It was established in 1792, and it has general supervision of all the branch mints. Can you name the locations of three of the four current mints?

Answer: Coins are currently minted in Denver, Colorado; San Francisco, California; Philadelphia, Pennsylvania; and West Point, New York. The Philadelphia mint was the first mint and has existed since 1793. All dies for United States coins are made there. Coins have been minted in San Francisco since 1854, in Denver since 1906, and in West Point only since 1984.

348 Name the capital of these South American countries:

A. Argentina
B. Chile
C. Venezuela

Answers: A. Buenos Aires
B. Santiago
C. Caracas

350 Can you give a word for each meaning below that begins with the letters *bob*?

A. a type of bird
B. something to ride in the snow
C. something to wear on your feet

Answers: A. *bobolink* or *bobwhite*
B. *bobsled*
C. *bobby socks*

349 Can you name three of the most visited national parks in the United States?

Possible answers:
1. Great Smoky Mountains National Park, North Carolina/Tennessee—9.3 million visitors in 1996
2. Grand Canyon National Park, Arizona—4.5 million visitors in 1996
3. Yosemite National Park, California—4 million visitors in 1996

351 Grandma is crocheting a striped afghan. It will have 16 stripes in all using three colors following this pattern: green, yellow, blue, green, yellow, blue, etc. If each stripe uses two ounces of yarn, how many ounces of each color of yarn will Grandma need?

Answer: There will be 6 green stripes, 5 yellow stripes, and 5 blue stripes. So Grandma will need 12 ounces of green, 10 ounces of yellow, and 10 ounces of blue.

352 How many countries can you name whose flags are completely red, white, and blue?

Possible answers: the United States, France, United Kingdom, Cambodia, Nepal, New Zealand, Australia, Luxembourg, Liberia, and others

---

353 What was the name of the Soviet space station launched in 1986?

Answer: The permanent station was named *Mir*, which is the Russian word for *peace*.

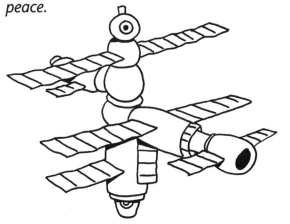

354 List at least three major works by Charles Dickens.

Possible answers: *Oliver Twist, A Christmas Carol, A Tale of Two Cities, Great Expectations, David Copperfield*

355 What is the only element named after one of the 50 United States?

Answer: Californium (symbol Cf) with an atomic weight of 98 was first synthesized in 1950 at the University of California at Berkeley.

---

356 What was the name given to the period after the U.S. Civil War when the nation was reunited and the economy restored?

Answer: It was called the Reconstruction and lasted from 1865 until about 1877.

357 If a room measuring 12' by 15' is to be covered with carpeting that costs $10 per square yard, how much will carpeting cost for the entire room?

Answer: The room has an area of 20 sq. yd., so the cost will be $200.

358 Which body of water does not border on the United States?
A. Gulf of Mexico   C. Hudson Bay
B. Pacific Ocean   D. Bering Sea

Answer: C. Hudson Bay is in part of Canada and does not touch the United States.

359 What country has the

A. greatest reserve of natural gas?
B. largest crude oil reserve?
C. most nuclear reactors?

Answers, according to figures from 1995:
A. Russia has the largest reserve at over 48 trillion cubic meters. Iran is second with 21 trillion.
B. Saudi Arabia at the end of 1995 had almost 36 billion metric tons. Second was Iraq with 13.4 billion.
C. The United States had the most at the end of 1995 with 108. France was second with 56, and Japan was third with 50.

360 What single word can precede each of these to complete three compound words?
A. smith, fish, finch
B. ball, cracker, fly
C. beat, set, spring

Answers: A. *gold*
         B. *fire*
         C. *off*

361 How did Legionnaire's disease get its name?

Answer: It was so named because it was first identified when it broke out at a convention of the American Legion in Philadelphia in 1976. It is caused by bacteria which breeds in warm water, and it causes a pneumonia-like illness.

---

362 What nickname is used to describe a left-handed baseball pitcher?

Answer: southpaw

363 Time on the planet of Marzook is quite different from time on Earth. One day on Marzook is as long as one week on Earth. How long in Earth time is one hour on Marzook?

Answer: One hour on Marzook would last as long as seven hours on Earth, since one day equals seven days.

---

364 Can you name a pair of homonyms (words that sound the same) for each set of definitions?
  A. a female sheep and a pronoun
  B. a manner of walking or running, and a barrier used to close an entrance through a wall or fence
  C. a person invited to a meal; formed a hypothesis about something

Answers: A. ewe/you
          B. gait/gate
          C. guest/guessed

---

365 Who was the first chief justice of the U.S. Supreme Court?

Answer: John Jay, who served 1789-1795.

366 The Ivy League is now the collective term for eight long-established U.S. universities. Originally there were just four members, the first four private universities on the East Coast. How did they become known as the "Ivy League"?

Answer: The name came from the pronunciation of IV, the Roman numeral for 4.

Can you name at least six of the eight universities in the Ivy League?

Answer: The eight are Harvard, Yale, Columbia, Brown, Princeton, Pennsylvania, Dartmouth, and Cornell.

PRINCEBIA   HARTON
YALVARD
COLMOUTH   PENNELL

367 If A x B = 24 and B x 5 = 15, then what numbers do A and B represent?

Answer: A = 8, B = 3

368 What state in the United States has the longest coastline?

Answer: Alaska has a coastline over 6,600 miles long, the longest in the United States.

369 Words like *face* and *media* are spelled using only letters from the first half of the alphabet, or the letters A to M. What words can you spell using only these same letters for each definition here?
  A. dreary
  B. a cloverlike plant
  C. a Caribbean country
  D. a state in the southern United States

Possible answers: A. bleak
                   B. alfalfa
                   C. Jamaica
                   D. Alabama

370 On the pH scale a number below 7 indicates an acid. A pH of exactly 7 (as in distilled water) indicates neutrality. What does a number above 7 indicate?

Answer: a base. It shows alkalinity. Weak alkalis such as soap measure 9 or 10. Corrosive alkalis such as lye have a pH of 13.

371 How many types of fish can you name that are spelled with five or fewer letters?

Possible answers: tuna, smelt, pike, cod, perch, shark, skate, eel, carp, ray, bass

How many types of fish can you name that are spelled with exactly seven letters?

Possible answers: herring, anchovy, catfish, sunfish, grouper

372 What is the mathematical term for a quantity that when multiplied by another equals 1, such as ½ when multiplied by 2?

Answer: It is called the *reciprocal*.

373 How many men's names can you list that begin with the letter C?

Possible answers: Carl, Craig, Clifford, Clint, Charles, Clive, Clyde, Carson, Curtis, Cameron, Clarence, Clem, Claude, Cecil, Cyrus

374 What was the name of the first artificial satellite, launched by the Soviet Union in 1957?

Answer: *Sputnik I* was launched on October 4, 1957, and carried only a simple radio transmitter which allowed scientists to track it as it orbited the earth. It burned up in the atmosphere 92 days later.

375 In what city would you find

A. Covent Garden and Trafalgar Square?
B. The Renaissance Center and Wayne State University?
C. The Gateway Arch?

Answers: A. London, England
B. Detroit, Michigan
C. St. Louis, Missouri

376 A string of Christmas tree lights is 8 feet long and has a bulb every 4 inches. What is the maximum number of lights on this string?

Answer: If there is a bulb at the very beginning of the string (at inch 0), and one every four inches thereafter (at inches 4, 8, 12, and so on), there would be 25 lights.

377 Which of these cities are located on the Atlantic coast? Boston, Charleston, Albany, Miami, Atlanta, Atlantic City

Answer: All but Albany and Atlanta are on the coast.

378 What is the capital of each of these Middle East countries?
A. Saudi Arabia
B. Lebanon
C. Jordan

Answer: A. Riyadh
B. Beirut
C. Amman

379 What branch of medicine is concerned with the study and treatment of the brain, spinal cord, and nerves?

Answer: neurology

380 Five neighbors live next to one another on the same street. Listen to find out who lives where:

Miss Daisy lives next to Miss Rose who lives next to the person in the house on the west end. Miss Daisy also lives next to Miss Pansy. Miss Tulip does not live next to Miss Rose, and Miss Lilac does not live next to Miss Pansy.

Tell the order in which the ladies live from west to east.

Answer: Miss Lilac, Miss Rose, Miss Daisy, Miss Pansy, Miss Tulip

---

381 Can you name two inventions for which Benjamin Franklin is credited?

Possible answers: lightning conductor, bifocal lenses

382 In Jupiter basketball, a field goal is worth 7 points and a free throw is worth 3 points.

A. Could a team score a total of 23 points? If so, how?

B. Is there a total between 20 and 30 points that is not possible to reach in Jupiter basketball?

Answer:
A. Yes, it is possible with two field goals (fg) and 3 free throws (ft).
B. All scores between 20 and 30 are possible. Here is one way for each score:

20–2fg, 2ft	24–3fg, 1ft	28–4fg
21–3fg	25–1fg, 6ft	29–2fg, 5ft
22–1fg, 5ft	26–2fg, 4ft	30–3fg, 3ft
23–2fg, 3ft	27–3fg, 2ft	

383 How many
A. acres are in one square mile?
B. feet are in three miles?
C. pints in five gallons?
D. ounces in one ton?

Answers:
A. 640 acres
B. 5,280 x 3 = 15,840 feet
C. 8 x 5 = 40 pints
D. 16 x 2,000 = 32,000 ounces

---

384 List ten or more words of four letters in which all the letters appear in reverse alphabetical order. The word *zone* is one example.

Possible answers: *tone, void, woke, sofa, tied, sole, some, pond, told, wife,* etc.

---

385 In Einstein's famous theory of relativity, $E = mc^2$, what does each of the letters represent?

Answer: E = energy, m = mass, c = speed of light in a vacuum

386 This year I am four times as old as my daughter. In 20 years, I will be twice as old as my daughter. What are our ages this year?

Answer: My age is 40; my daughter's age is 10.

387 Name at least seven infectious (contagious) diseases.

Possible answers: cold, influenza, chicken pox, measles, mumps, mononucleosis, tuberculosis, meningitis, etc.

388 Try to answer these literature trivia questions:

A. On what London street did Sherlock Holmes live?

B. What were the names of E. B. White's famous spider and pig?

C. When soap failed, how was Peter Pan's shadow reattached?

D. What was Gulliver's profession in *Gulliver's Travels?*

Answers: A. Baker Street
B. Charlotte and Wilbur
C. Wendy sewed it on.
D. He was a ship's physician.

---

389 There are 6 zops in 1 zup and 2 zups in 1 zype.

A. How many zops are in 3 zypes?

B. How many zypes are in 12 zups?

Answers: A. 3 zypes = 6 zups = 36 zops
B. Since 2 zups = 1 zype, then 12 zups = 6 zypes.

390 Visualize the 26 letters of the alphabet written in a single row from A to Z.

A. Starting at the A and moving forward, can you "see" any three-letter words, spelled by letters in consecutive order? If so, what are they?

B. Now try to picture the same alphabet in reverse, from Z to A. Again, can you see any three-letter words? What are they?

C. Finally, check in both directions for two-letter words. What can you find?

Answers: For all questions, you need only to check the letters around the A, E, I, O, U, and Y since every word must contain a vowel.

A. no words

B. *fed*

C. going forward: *hi, no;* in reverse: *on*

391 If day 1 of a 30-day cruise is on a Wednesday, on what day of the week would be day 30?

Answer: It would be on a Thursday. The 29th day would be a Wednesday, four weeks after the beginning of the cruise. The next day, day 30, would then be on a Thursday.

392 Many words have double meanings. For example, the work *club* can refer to a group that meets together or to a weapon. What double-meaning word is referred to in each description here?

A. a kind of fish, the bottom of a shoe
B. a short note, a string
C. a furnace, to counterfeit
D. a floor covering, a border

Answers: A. sole
B. line
C. forge
D. mat

393 In what city and state are each of these famous U.S. institutions of higher learning located?

A. University of Notre Dame
B. Yale University
C. Johns Hopkins University

Answers: A. Notre Dame, Indiana
B. New Haven, Connecticut
C. Baltimore, Maryland

394 The calendar year can be divided into four quarters. January through March, April through June, July through September, and October through December. Assume this is not a leap year.

A. Which one of these three-month periods contains exactly 91 days?
B. Which two of these periods combined contain exactly 184 days?

Answers: A. April-June
B. July-September and October-December

395 Listen to this sentence. Tell how many times the letter S appears in it. "She asked how to shear sheep successfully with scissors."

Answer: 11

---

396 What is *hemophilia?*

Answer: It is an inherited disease in which normal blood clotting is impaired. A person with this disease is known as a *hemophiliac.* He/she experiences prolonged bleeding from the slightest wound.

---

397 In 1913 a popular baseball player named Luis Francis Sockalexis died. He had been the first American Indian ever to play professional baseball, and the team was named in his honor. What is the current name of this baseball team?

Answer: The team is the Cleveland Indians, previously known as the Naps, the Spiders, and other names.

398 Which U.S. president was the only one to serve two nonconsecutive terms?

Answer: Grover Cleveland was both the twenty-second and the twenty-fourth president. He served from 1885 to 1889 and from 1893 to 1897. Benjamin Harrison served as president between those two terms.

---

399 A lone contestant on Jeopardy correctly answers all the questions in one category, from $100 to $500. How much money did she win for that category?

Answer: $100 + $200 + $300 + $400 + $500 = $1500

Questions only I know the answers to for $300, Alex.

400 Which planet is the seventh from the sun?

Answer: Uranus

---

401 What musical instrument is a set of bars arranged like a piano keyboard? Its longer bars play deeper notes when struck with a mallet.

Answer: a xylophone or marimba

---

402 What is the name given to the scale used to measure the strength of the waves from earthquakes?

Answer: The Richter scale was named after Charles Francis Richter who devised it. He lived from 1900 to 1985.

403 Can you name a pair of rhyming words for each set of definitions?
A. to use sparingly; small, edible crustaceans
B. to stare stupidly at something; a large bird of prey
C. wriggle; fixed and stable
D. hard-wearing cotton fabric; poisonous fluid from snakes

Answers: A. scrimp, shrimp
B. gawk, hawk
C. squirm, firm
D. denim, venom

---

404 Name the state with each of these nicknames:
A. Treasure State   C. Empire State
B. Equality State   D. Keystone State

Answers: A. Montana
B. Wyoming
C. New York
D. Pennsylvania

405 The Smith family owns 2 cars, 4 bicycles, 1 unicycle, and 2 tricycles. How many tires are there in all?

Answer: (2 x 4) + (4 x 2) + 1 + (2 x 3) = 23

---

406 Which of these cities are located on the Great Lakes? Buffalo, Cleveland, Detroit, Indianapolis, Chicago, Milwaukee, St. Paul

Answer: Indianapolis and St. Paul are not located on the Great Lakes.

---

407 What is the name for the technique used in oil painting in which small spots of pure color are dabbed side by side to create in the viewer's eye an impression of blended colors?

Answer: It is called *pointillism*. It was developed in the 1880s by Seurat, a Neo-Impressionist.

408 Name the capital of each of these Pacific countries:
A. Australia
B. Indonesia
C. Philippines

Answers: A. Canberra
B. Jakarta
C. Manila

---

409 What city has the most skyscrapers in the world?

Answer: New York City has the most with 131. Chicago is second with 47, and Hong Kong is third with 30.

410 We use many common phrases that include items of food. For example, we say that something is *not our cup of tea* or that something is *flat as a pancake*. Try to list at least five more phrases that mention something edible.

Possible answers: the apple of his eye, bringing home the bacon, cool as a cucumber, spilling the beans, going bananas, proof of the pudding, etc.

411 What base 10 numerals are equal to these base 2 (binary) numerals?

A. 11_2

B. 1100_2

C. 10110_2

Answers: A. 3
            B. 12
            C. 22

412 If all of these writers were alive today, who would be the oldest? Youngest?

A. Robert Frost
B. Agatha Christie
C. Robert Louis Stevenson
D. Mark Twain

Answers: Mark Twain would be the oldest; Agatha Christie would be the youngest. The birth year of each in chronological order is: Twain–1835, Stevenson–1850, Frost–1874, Christie–1890.

413 Name at least two books written by Robert Louis Stevenson.

Possible answers: *Kidnapped, Treasure Island, Dr. Jekyll and Mr. Hyde, A Child's Garden of Verses,* and *The Master of Ballantrae*

414 What is the only man-made structure on earth that can be seen from space?

Answer: the Great Wall of China. It is 4,000 miles long with all its branches.

415 Martha Jane Burke was better known by her nickname. She was a legendary shooter, horserider, and scout, born in South Dakota around 1852. By what name was she known?

Answer: Calamity Jane. She is remembered especially for the time she spent in the Black Hills of Dakota during the 1870 gold rush.

416 Which of these is not a major city in Germany?

A. Frankfurt   C. Salzburg
B. Munich   D. Hamburg

Answer: C. Salzburg is in Austria.

417 In one 24-hour day, Luke spends $\frac{1}{3}$ of his time asleep, $\frac{1}{4}$ of his time in school, and $\frac{1}{12}$ of his time doing homework. How many hours does Luke have free for everything else?

Answer: 8 hours. Luke spends 8 hours asleep, 6 hours in school, and 2 hours doing homework. That leaves 8 of his 24 hours free.

418 Name at least six different parts of computer hardware.

Possible answers: circuit board, power supply, the monitor, keyboard, disk drive, printer, the housing unit

419 What is the name of the single currency being adopted by several different European countries?

Answer: the Euro. It allows member nations to buy and sell goods without concern about varying exchange rates among different currencies.

420 What Republican candidate ran against Bill Clinton for U.S. President in 1992? In 1996?

Answers: In 1992 it was then-president George Bush. In 1996 it was Bob Dole.

---

421 What tropical grass is used both for eating and making furniture?

Answer: bamboo. Some species grow as tall as 120 feet. The stems are hollow and jointed and can be used in the construction of furniture, houses, and boats. The young shoots are edible.

422 Estimate how much money the Jones family spends on peanut butter and jelly sandwiches for one year. The Joneses buy 2 loaves of bread per week at an average cost of $1.50 per loaf. They buy 3 jars of peanut butter per month at a cost of $3 per jar. They buy 2 jars of jelly per month at a cost of $2 per jar. What is the family's yearly expense?

Answer: It is about $300 per year. Bread: $3/week x about 50 weeks = $150; Peanut Butter: $9/month x 12 months = $108; Jelly: $4/month x 12 months = $48.

---

423 What island was formerly known as Formosa?

Answer: Taiwan. It was first settled by China in the fifteenth century. Since then it has been under control of the Dutch, then the Japanese, and then it was regained by the Chinese after World War II.

---

424 What single English word can refer to: a waterproof layer of the stems and roots of trees, a bottle stopper, and an Irish seaport?

Answer: cork/Cork

425 Name the capital of each of these Canadian provinces.

A. Ontario
B. Alberta
C. Nova Scotia

Answers: A. Toronto
B. Edmonton
C. Halifax

426 Words like *tons* and *vow* are spelled using only letters from the last half of the alphabet, from N to Z. What words can you spell using these same letters for each definition here?

A. most awful
B. a plant with brightly colored flowers
C. a utensil
D. to strengthen or reinforce

Possible answers: A. worst
B. poppy
C. spoon
D. support

427 What astronomer is best known for his belief that the sun, not the earth, is the center of the solar system?

Answer: Copernicus. He was born in Poland in 1473. For 30 years he worked on his hypotheses of the rotation and orbital motion of earth. His writing, *About the Revolutions of the Heavenly Spheres,* was published in 1543, the year of his death.

428 Briefly explain the law of double jeopardy.

Answer: It is the principle that a person cannot be prosecuted twice for the same offense. It is contained in the Fifth Amendment of the U.S. Constitution.

429 Who was the author of *Charlie and the Chocolate Factory?* Can you name at least two other books by the same author?

Answers: The author was Roald Dahl, who also wrote *Matilda; James and the Giant Peach; The Twits; Tales of the Unexpected; Giraffe, Pelly, and Me;* and many, many others.

430 How would you write these base ten numbers in base two, or the binary system?
A. 10
B. 20
C. 35

Answers: A. 1010_2
B. 10100_2
C. 100011_2

431 What U.S. president became a Supreme Court justice after finishing his presidency?

Answer: William Howard Taft was Chief Justice from 1921 to 1930.

432 Which country does not share a border with Egypt?
A. Libya   C. Jordan
B. Algeria   D. Sudan

Answer: B. Algeria does not border Egypt; Libya is located between the two countries.

433 In what part of the human body would you find the humerus, radius, and ulna?

Answer: These are all names of bones in the arm. The humerus is the long bone in the upper arm, while the other two are in the lower arm.

434 **What is the probability of getting two red socks in two draws from a pile of three red socks and three white socks?**

Answer: You have a probability of $\frac{2}{6}$ of drawing a red sock the first time, followed by a probability of $\frac{1}{5}$ of drawing a red one the second time. So to get two red socks in two draws, the probability is $\frac{2}{6} \times \frac{1}{5}$, or $\frac{1}{15}$.

435 **Name two Disney feature-length cartoons made before 1960.**

Possible answers: *Snow White and the Seven Dwarfs* (1938), *Pinocchio* (1939), *Fantasia* (1940), *Dumbo* (1941), and *Bambi* (1942)

436 **Name at least three bodies of water that touch the continent of Africa.**

Possible answers: Mediterranean Sea, Atlantic Ocean, Indian Ocean, Red Sea

437 **To which of the five senses does each adjective refer?**

A. auditory **C. tactile**
B. gustatory **D. olfactory**

Answers: A. hearing
B. tasting
C. touching
D. smelling

438 **What do the letters HTML stand for?**

Answer: HyperText Markup Language. It is a computer language used in making web pages.

439 Which is larger, the cube root of 343, or the square root of 81?

Answer: The square root of 81 (9) is larger than the cube root of 343 (7).

---

440 What is measured by each of these instruments?

A. hygrometer
B. barometer
C. pedometer

Answers:
A. This measures humidity or water vapor content of a gas, usually air.
B. A barometer measures atmospheric pressure as an indication of weather.
C. This measures the approximate distance covered by a person walking.

441 Which state in the United States is most densely populated? Which is least densely populated?

Answers: New Jersey is the most with a population of about 7.7 million in an area of less than 7,800 square miles. Alaska is the least with a population of just over 0.5 million in an area of 591,000 square miles.

442 What do the letters CAD and CAM stand for?

Answer: CAD stands for Computer-Aided Design. It is the use of computers for creating and editing design drawings used widely in architecture, electronics, and engineering. CAM stands for Computer-Aided Manufacturing, which is the use of computers to control production processes. Often this involves the control of machine tools and robots. In some factories, the whole design and production system has been automated by linking CAD to CAM.